To MY DAD who popped the corn and to Mom who got the books to read for our popcorn parties long ago . . .

**By Carolyn Vosburg Hall
and the Food Editors of *Farm Journal***

Illustrations by the author

DOUBLEDAY & COMPANY, INC.
Garden City, New York

The author collected technical information and
helpful ideas about popcorn from the United States
Department of Agriculture; the Iowa Crop and
Livestock Reporting Service; The Encyclopedia of
Food; Gerald Lee of the B&L Popcorn Company;
The Popcorn Institute; James Trelore of the *Detroit
News;* Keith Kline, who is curator of birds at the
Detroit Zoological Park; *Farm Journal* agronomist
Gary Reynolds; and the Food Editors of *Farm
Journal,* who tested and perfected all recipes and
contributed information on nutrition. Thanks to
Florence Bowman, secretary.

ISBN: 0-385-11049-9 Trade
       0-385-11050-2 Prebound
Library of Congress Catalog Card Number 75–36593

About Popcorn

Popcorn is a natural food. It is not a candy or dessert or breakfast cereal but it can be used as any one of them. The corn you buy in the store was grown in a farmer's field, dried just right, and then packaged by a popcorn company to keep it moist and fresh for delivery to you. Nothing is added or taken away. It's pure. You can even grow it yourself (directions on pages 62–63).

Popcorn grows like all other corn. Cobs full of kernels, called "ears," grow on tall stalks in fields and gardens. The popcorn kernel is smaller and harder than sweet corn or field corn. It contains mostly hard starch, which makes it pop better than any other kind of corn. Corn grown for grinding won't pop at all because it is practically all soft starch.

Scientists agree that popcorn was our first corn. The Indians must have discovered the magic of it thousands of years ago, when a wild popcorn kernel was accidentally exposed to heat. Suddenly, this hard kernel was tender and tasty and easy to eat! Probably the earliest way of popping corn was to throw it into a bed of hot coals and catch what popped out.

Popping popcorn is a fun and easy way to "cook" something good. You get quick results: wildly popping corn, ready in minutes for a crunchy feast.

As a snack, popcorn is a natural "energy food," like fruit. Starches and sugars (which are called carbohydrates) are the major source of energy in our diets. Popcorn is three-quarters starch. And while it doesn't have all the vitamins that fruit has, popcorn does give you some protein and other nutrients. As for calories, one cup of unbuttered popped corn has fewer calories than an orange.

But who can stop at only one cup of popcorn? Not me! We munch down more than four hundred million pounds of popcorn in this country every year. That means about two pounds apiece . . . or enough to fill thirty-two quart bowls when it's popped.

If you're going to eat your share, you'll like the new ideas in this book for flavoring and serving this popular snack. You'll find twenty-five ways to use popcorn . . . easy recipes and directions first, and then the fancy stuff.

Enjoy!

25 ways to fix popcorn

1. Private Popcorn Party
2. Buttery Popcorn
3. Movie Popcorn
4. Campfire Popcorn
5. Spanish Popcorn
6. Peruvian Popcorn
7. Breakfast Bonanza
8. Peanut Butter Popcorn
9. Crunchy Lunch
10. Finger-food Snack Supper
11. Crunchies
12. Munchies
13. Wow Your Friends
14. Party Popcorn
15. Pizza Popcorn
16. Easy Caramel Corn
17. Trick or Treat
18. Popcorn Sculpture
19. Summer Suckers
20. Easter Eggs
21. Happy Birthday
22. Chocolate Popcorn Bars
23. Hawaiian Popcorn Bars
24. Popcorn Fudge
25. Croutons and Experiment

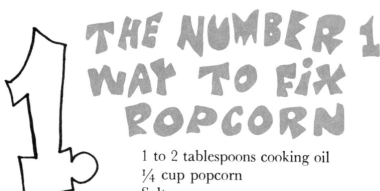

THE NUMBER 1 WAY TO FIX POPCORN

1 to 2 tablespoons cooking oil
¼ cup popcorn
Salt

Popping Directions:

1. This recipe makes about 1 quart of popped corn. But it needs plenty of room to pop, so use a heavy saucepan, 2 quarts or bigger, with a close-fitting lid. (If you have a popcorn popper, follow its directions.)

2. Pour enough oil in the pan to cover the bottom. Heat on medium to high temperature. Drop two test kernels into the pan. When the test kernels pop, add the rest of the popcorn. (Kernels should barely cover the bottom of the pan, no more than one kernel deep.)

3. Pick up your pot holders and hold the lid on tight while you shake the pan over the heat. Shaking the kernels in the hot oil helps heat them quickly and evenly, so they pop better and don't burn. Corn should start popping in a minute or two, and be done in another minute.

4. Pour the popcorn into a bowl. Salt to your taste. Add a good book, a cold drink and a soft seat for your private popcorn party.

To make a full batch of popcorn, double the recipe. Use 2 to 3 tablespoons cooking oil, ½ cup popcorn and a 3- or 4-quart saucepan or Dutch oven.

FOR A PRIVATE POPCORN PARTY

I love popcorn.
I like to hear it popping in
the pan and crunching
in my mouth. I like
the warm bowl and
the salty flavor.

WHAT is GOING ON IN THERE?

Popcorn explodes! Inside the hard flinty kernel, there's moisture and a tiny soft core. When you heat popcorn, the moisture turns to steam. The hard starch holds in the steam until it finally builds up enough pressure and power to blast through. The explosion turns the kernel inside out, puffing it up to about thirty times its original size. Pop half a cup of kernels and you'll get 2 quarts or more of popcorn. How's that for magic?

HARD STARCH

SOFT STARCH

POPCORN pops

field corn can't pop

2. Buttery Popcorn

1 batch popped corn (about 2 quarts)
3 tablespoons butter
Salt

Melt the butter carefully in a pan over low heat so it will not burn. Drizzle it over the popcorn and stir with a long spoon or shake it in a big bowl or pan to coat all the kernels. Sprinkle with salt.

Popcorn & Butter go together like Cows & Corn on the farm.

Cows love all kinds of corn, including popcorn. That's why farmers put fences around fields of corn —to keep the cows out.

When popcorn ripens, farmers pick the ears and store them in corn cribs to finish drying. Then they often open the fence gate and let the cows into the field to eat what's left on the cornstalks.

Eating corn helps cows give milk, which the farmer sells to a dairy. Dairymen separate cream from the milk and churn it into butter to pour on your popcorn. Cows and popcorn go together from field to feast.

Did you know that there are Several Kinds of Popcorn?

When you grocery shop for popcorn, you'll find at least two kinds: yellow pearl and smaller white rice-shaped kernels. The white popcorn, called hulless, has thin hulls so no tough skins will stick in your teeth. Some kinds of yellow popcorn are "hulless" too, but the biggest puffers have some hulls. Movie theaters pop the biggest "butterflies" they can get, to fill up the boxes. One special yellow kernel pops to forty-four times its size! Most pop about thirty-two times bigger. The white pops only about twenty-five times its size, but many people like the taste better. The big round yellow "mushroom" variety is used for caramel corn.

The most unusual varieties of popcorn grow colored kernels—red, blue, white, yellow, calico and brown—but they all pop white. Popcorn growers are always working to develop even more hybrid varieties that will pop better and taste better.

MOVIE POPCORN

3.

½ cup large yellow popcorn per movie
¼ cup peanut or corn oil
Butter salt

Pop the corn in a pan or popper and pour it into a double grocery bag. It's got a wide mouth to pour into. Do you? The heavy paper bag keeps the popcorn warm longer during the movie.

Butter salt was developed for movie popcorn. It is finely ground so it clings to the popcorn and doesn't settle to the bottom. It has a buttery flavor but isn't as smeary as butter. You can find it in jars at the grocery or packed in some packages of popcorn.

Theater managers know that selling popcorn at the movies pleases their customers and helps their business.

I LOVE TO COOK BECAUSE I LOVE TO EAT

OK. I'M READY

Cooking is exciting, fun and easy to learn. But some of that stuff in the kitchen is dangerous. Here's how to cope with the kitchen without getting hurt, ruining the food or wrecking the place.

Hot. How hot do you think popcorn has to get before it pops? Would you believe 250 degrees hotter than boiling water? If you've never popped corn or worked at the stove, ask an experienced cook like Mom or Dad to stand by when you make popcorn the first time.

Stoves and Poppers. Always use pot holders to protect your hands when you touch hot pots. Turn the pan handles in on the stove so they won't be knocked plop on the floor. And keep the appliance cords well back on the counter so nobody tangles with them. When you move a hot pan off the stove, set it on a hot pad or trivet so it will not burn the counter top.

I DIDN'T plan this!

Directions. Recipes tell you what tools and foods to use. Put them all out before you start . . . cooking pans, measuring spoons and cups, mixing bowls, everything. Measure all the ingredients and line them up, ready to grab when you need them. Follow the recipe carefully. You can make changes, more salt or less butter, after you've tried it. Put away supplies after you've measured what you need. That keeps your work counter clear.

Clean-up. Keep a clean-up cloth, sponge or paper towel handy to wipe up what spills. Who likes to work on a messy counter? And a wet slippery floor is dangerous.

Wipe the Wet. Dry your hands often. Wet hands drop things. Professional chefs hang a towel from their waists to use all the time. Never touch electric appliances or cords with wet hands. You could get a bad shock!

Be Prepared. Talk with your parents about working safely in the kitchen—what to do if the cooking fat catches fire or you burn your finger. If you think about accidents that might happen, often you can prevent them. Like all craftsmen, good cooks take pride in learning how to use and care for their tools and work space. Okay. Now begin. And soon you'll be an artist in

THE ART OF COOKING

Popcorn lovers have their favorite pans for the popping ceremony. Grandmothers often prefer an old familiar saucepan worn from shaking on the stove. Kids like the electric popper or fondue pot with non-stick finish because it's easy to clean, you don't need a stove and the popcorn is less likely to burn. Campers like a frying pan because it is the only pan they brought, or a wire popper because it is lightweight and easy to carry.

Ancient poppers were made of clay. Some pots had the opening in the side, and stood over the fire on three legs. The Papago Indians of Arizona still pop corn in shallow clay *ollas* as much as eight feet wide. Winnebago Indians didn't even use a pan. They pushed a stick into the whole ear of corn and held it over the fire.

The best pans for popping corn have heavy bottoms that spread the heat evenly. Some new electric poppers have high, see-through plastic covers with a butter-melting place on top. You will find a "Seal of Approval" on poppers tested and okayed by the Popcorn Institute.

A modern jiffy-pop invention sells corn, butter and salt sealed into a disposable pan with a foil lid that blows up like a balloon as the popcorn expands. Newest of all is a popcorn packet that pops in a microwave oven in seconds.

24 Camp Fire Popcorn

½ cup yellow popcorn
Wire popper
Butter salt or butter and salt

Put corn in wire popper, slide top shut. Shake over campfire until kernels are popped. Since this corn is popped without oil, it will be very dry. Pour melted butter on for moisture and taste, if you brought it. Salt as you like.

POPCORN is HEAVENLY

5

2 quarts unsalted popped corn
1 cup salted Spanish peanuts
3 tablespoons butter
1 teaspoon garlic salad dressing mix
(in foil packet)

Pop the corn. Mix it with the peanuts in a bowl.
(If you use a deep bowl, popcorn will stay warm
longer.) Melt the butter over low heat. Pour it over
the popcorn and peanuts and stir or toss to mix it
up. Sprinkle with salad dressing. Mix again.

The ancient Peruvians of South America called corn the Gift of the Gods. No one knows for sure where it developed first, in North or South America. The tiny kernels found in the Bat Cave in Mexico may be as old as 5,600 years. That's old! Scientists are sure that the earliest cultivated corn was popcorn.

Nearly all the Indian tribes of North and South America were eating popped corn and using it for decoration—for headdresses and necklaces—long before the European settlers came here. American Indians brought popcorn to the Pilgrims, their gift for the first Thanksgiving feast.

 2 quarts unsalted popped corn
¼ cup butter
½ teaspoon sage
½ teaspoon salt
½ teaspoon onion powder
⅛ teaspoon seasoned pepper

Pop the corn. Melt the butter over low heat. Pour over popcorn and mix well. Sprinkle on seasonings and mix again. MMMM!

Breakfast Bonanza

7. Pop a small amount of corn and pour into a cereal bowl. Put on a little salt, brown sugar and milk. Eat it before it gets soggy, unless you like it that way.

One of the healthiest ways to eat popcorn is with dairy products like milk, butter or cheese. The earliest settlers ate popped corn for breakfast. The colonial women served it as the first puffed cereal. This corn given by the Indians, helped the Pilgrims to survive those first harsh winters in America. The Indians also showed the settlers how to plant and grow the corn. After drying in the sun and air, popcorn stored well over the winter.

Now, most of our popcorn is grown in the "Corn Belt"—those midwestern states where the climate and soil are just right for raising all kinds of corn. Farmers in Indiana and Iowa plant the most popcorn. Next come Nebraska, Ohio, Kansas, Kentucky, Michigan and Missouri. But popcorn can be grown in all other states too.

While corn is a major United States crop, only a small portion of it is *pop*corn. The rest is field corn or sweet corn, both of which were developed from the original popcorn.

LET'S MUNCH A CRUNCHY LUNCH

We Americans love variety in our meals. We eat more different kinds of foods than people in most other countries of the world. For a different lunch in the old brown bag, how about peanut butter popcorn?

8.

2 quarts unsalted popped corn
¼ cup butter
¼ cup peanut butter

Melt the butter and add the peanut butter to it. Stir until smooth and pour the butters over the hot popped corn. Toss to mix and serve warm. Nutty flavor . . . good!

9.

1 (2½-ounce) jar or package dried beef
½ cup butter (1 stick)
½ cup chopped celery
3 quarts unsalted popped corn

Chop the dried beef into small pieces. Melt the butter in a frying pan over low heat. Stir beef bits into the butter, and fry gently for a few minutes. Put warm popcorn and chopped celery in a bowl. Pour on butter and beef mixture and toss to mix. Neat-O!

I LOVE POPCORN

And popcorn loves you back—it gives you pep and zip (energy). Energy, figured in calories, is the first thing your body needs to be alive. You need energy to make use of the other nutrients in food . . . to breathe, to digest what you eat, and put it to work building muscles, brains and blood. You need even more energy to ride a bike or race your dog.

So think of popcorn as "go" food. It's three-quarters starch (carbohydrates). While you'll get most of your protein from other foods, popcorn has a small amount of protein to help build muscles and fight diseases. There are small amounts of other nutrients in popcorn too: calcium and iron for strong bones and red blood; and the B vitamins riboflavin (to grow and see better) and niacin (to smooth out your feelings and your skin too).

Popcorn is a carbohydrate snack that doesn't decay your teeth, because it's starchy and chewy instead of sugary and sticky.

You don't need to read this page, you can just show it to your mom to let her know how

GOOD

POPCORN is for you!

What about calories? We measure popcorn's energy value in terms of calories. One cup of popped corn (popped in cooking oil, but not buttered) has 54 calories. Compare that with a frosted chocolate cupcake at 120 calories!

If you pour on melted butter, you pour on more calories. Ounce for ounce, fats have more than twice the energy value (calories) than carbohydrates or proteins have. If you eat more calories than you can use, your body stores the surplus as fat. It is neither popular nor healthy to be too fat. So store extra calories in the kitchen until you need them.

There's one more nice thing about popcorn: its "mechanical" value. The flinty bits of the hull you see hiding in a popped kernel are indigestible carbohydrate, chiefly cellulose. Our bodies need some of this bulk and fiber (called roughage) to keep our systems working.

Finger Food Snack Supper

Sunday night supper in front of the TV calls for some kind of popcorn. Try this one . . . it's yummy.

10

2 tablespoons sugar
$\frac{1}{8}$ teaspoon ground cinnamon
$\frac{1}{8}$ teaspoon ground nutmeg
$\frac{1}{4}$ cup melted butter
2 quarts salted popped corn

Combine the sugar, cinnamon and nutmeg in a bowl. Melt the butter in a pan. Pour the butter over warm popped corn, stirring it with a wooden spoon to coat all the kernels. Sprinkle the sugar and spice mixture over the buttered popped corn. Serve in a big bowl. Or give each person a small bowl.

Complete the meal with other finger-food treats. Fruits and vegetables are great. Whole cherry tomatoes, orange segments, sliced apples, bananas, celery, peaches—whatever is in season. Little sausages or pieces of ham, sliced luncheon meat or cheese cubes on toothpicks go well with this meal. Arrange them all on a big tray —they'll look as good as they taste.

Pick-and-choose meals are nice.

CRUNCHIES and

⅓ cup butter
1 teaspoon Worcestershire sauce
¼ teaspoon garlic salt
6 cups unsalted popped corn
2 cups rice cereal squares
1 cup thin pretzel sticks

1. Melt the butter in a small pan and stir in the seasonings.

2. Drizzle this mixture over the popcorn, cereal squares and pretzel sticks in a big bowl, stirring to get them all coated with the butter.

3. Spread the mix in a large, shallow baking pan and put it in a preheated 250-degree oven to bake for 45 minutes. Stir it with a wooden spoon four or five times while it's baking.

This great party treat is less expensive than nuts or candy—and great for you.

MUNCHIES

4 quarts unsalted popped corn
1 (8-ounce) package pretzel rings
1 (3-ounce) package cheese curls
½ cup butter (1 stick)
1 teaspoon Worcestershire sauce
1 teaspoon celery salt

1. Mix up the popped corn, pretzels and cheese curls in a large roasting pan.

2. Melt the butter and stir in Worcestershire sauce. Pour over popcorn mixture, tossing lightly until mixed. Sprinkle with celery salt.

3. Bake in a preheated 250-degree oven for 45 minutes. Stir it up four or five times while it bakes.

You can fool around with any number of changes or substitutes in these two recipes. You can use garlic salt, or onion salt, or oregano, or more Worcestershire sauce or whatever you think might taste good. But there is an old Cook's Rule you don't experiment on company. Try it on the family first.

TENDER TEETH

ITEM: Dr. I. Pullem Teeth, Dentist, tells about an older patient of his who came in often to have teeth fixed that she broke while eating popcorn. He suggested she stop eating popcorn. She never came back.

For extra tender popcorn that is easier on tender teeth, pop the yellow or white popcorn in the regular way. Sort out any unpopped kernels and discard them. Butter a large shallow baking pan and spread the popped corn on it. Bake the popcorn in a preheated oven set at 250 degrees for an hour or more. (It is hard to smell popcorn for that long without having some.) After baking, the corn will be dry and tender.

my, you look tender!

I am.

So am I.

It didn't pop right!

1. If your popcorn has dried out, it won't pop well. To fix it, fill a quart jar ¾ full of popcorn and add 1 or 2 tablespoons of water. Tighten the jar lid and shake the corn often until it absorbs the water. Keep the jar sealed for two more days before you try to pop the corn. If your corn is very dry, do it again.

Corn pops best at 13.5 per cent moisture, and that's what farmers and processors aim for. Farmers let popcorn dry naturally on the stalk in the field. After picking, they either put the ears in corn cribs to finish drying; or they truck the corn to market. Processors test the corn's moisture and dry it further if necessary; they also clean, polish, grade and package it for you—just right for popping. To keep your corn fresh, store it in a tightly sealed glass jar, plastic bag or kitchen canister.

2. If your popcorn puffs are small, you may not have used enough oil in your pan. Oil conducts heat and makes the kernels pop bigger. But too much oil makes them greasy.

3. If your popcorn burns, the heat is too high. Or you didn't shake the pan enough.

4. If popcorn seems soggy maybe your pan lid fits too tightly and steam can't escape. Moisture condenses on the lid and drips. Take the lid off as soon as popping stops—try not to shake the drips into the corn.

WOW YOUR FRIENDS

Who doesn't like to nibble on a treat while playing games or cards? Serve napkins with this one to keep the games clean. If it's too sticky, bake it a few minutes longer.

13

Grated peel of 1 lemon
¼ cup sugar
3 tablespoons butter
4 quarts salted popped corn

1. To grate the lemon, wash and dry it first. Rub it against a fine grater, over a piece of waxed paper. Grate only the yellow part—the white has a bitter taste. Mix lemon peel and sugar together.

2. Melt the butter and pour it over popped corn in a large roasting pan. Sprinkle with lemon-sugar mixture. Toss lightly to mix.

3. Bake popcorn for 10 minutes in a preheated 350-degree oven.

PARTY POPCORN

"Say, George, this is great stuff. How do you get it out of your teeth?"

14

½ cup butter
½ cup brown sugar, firmly packed
3 quarts unsalted popped corn
1 cup pecan halves or mixed nuts

1. If butter is hard, let it soften to room temperature. Cream it—that means stir and beat it until it's smooth and creamy. Add brown sugar and beat them together until fluffy.

2. Combine popcorn and nuts in a bowl. Add butter mixture and mix with your hands to coat all the kernels and nuts.

3. Spread in a large roasting pan and bake in a preheated 350-degree oven about 10 minutes.

PIZZA POPCORN
for what'll I serve?

15
¼ cup butter (½ stick)
2 quarts unsalted popped corn
1 teaspoon Italian salad dressing
   mix (from a foil packet)

Melt the butter carefully over low heat. Pour it
over warm popped corn. Sprinkle with Italian salad
dressing mix. Toss gently to mix. Serve warm.

Save the rest of the salad dressing mix in its foil
packet to use the next time you want Pizza Popcorn.

you don't have to eat it. DECORATE YOUR CHRISTMAS TREE

You can string popcorn and fresh cranberries together to make garlands for your Christmas tree. Many people did this in the past before it became so easy to buy ornaments and tinsels in the stores.

The birds and squirrels will love to find a tree outside decorated for them. If you load the branches with strands of popcorn and cranberries, you'll see the birds gather to peck their breakfast.

The giant yellow popcorn that is a day old is easier to string than fresh popped corn or the smaller white corn. Use a large sharp needle and a fine strong thread that won't break the corn. Eat the ones that break.

"Maybe I can rattle a few presents while I am here."

Caramel corn and Cracker Jacks

Popcorn and candy make a tasty combination. The earliest popcorn popped into small white kernels with stiff skins or hulls. It tasted great but was tough to chew. A candy and popcorn company got the idea back in 1896 of coating popcorn and peanuts with molasses and corn syrup. A salesman tasted the concoction and exclaimed, "That's a crackajack!" "Crackajack" is an old-time expression, meaning something like "a great guy" does now. People also used the word to describe anything that was a winner. So the candy and popcorn company registered the name "Cracker Jack" as a trademark for their new confection. They still use the same recipe to make the boxed treat with the surprise inside.

In 1930, a new variety of giant yellow popcorn started the caramel corn fad. Caramel corn stores popped up everywhere. Of course, this sold a lot more popcorn.

EASY CARAMEL CORN

16 ¼ pound light caramel candy
2 tablespoons water
2 quarts salted popped corn

Put the candy and water in a heavy saucepan and melt the caramels slowly and carefully over low heat, stirring constantly with a wooden spoon. (Or put candy and water in a double boiler and melt over hot water—this takes longer, but it's safer.) When it makes a smooth sauce, pour it over the popped corn and stir to coat all the kernels. Spread it on a lightly buttered baking sheet to cool. Break into small chunks to eat.

popped art

Candied popcorn looks delightful and tastes divine. And the fun part is that it can be molded into sculpture that you can eat. What shapes can you think of to make?

The next seven recipes tell you how to make different flavors of candy syrup to pour over popcorn in order to shape it. If you cook it just right, the hot sticky syrup will harden as it cools, holding the popcorn together. Always pour hot syrup over warm popcorn—it coats more evenly.

Ask family and friends to help you. These recipes divide easily into parts so the fun can be shared.

Testing candy. Candy syrup expands a lot when it boils, so use a big saucepan. If your pan is too small, it will boil over. And boiling sugar is *extremely hot*. You need practice to cook candy to just the right stage or temperature. It's a good idea to get help from an experienced cook until you learn how to work with hot syrup.

The sure way to know when syrup is ready to pour is to use a candy thermometer. Recipes tell you what temperature it should be.

If you don't have a candy thermometer, use the cold water test. Fill a cup half full of cold water. After the syrup has boiled for about 10 or 15 minutes, carefully dip out about ½ teaspoonful of syrup and drop it off the spoon into the water.

The cold water will cool the syrup so you can touch it. See if you can form it into a ball with your fingertips. The longer you cook syrup, the harder the ball will get. For some recipes, you want it so hard it forms brittle threads. Each recipe will tell you at what stage to stop the cooking and pour the syrup.

Gather your helpers around you to make popcorn balls. When hot syrup starts to cool enough so you can touch it, it also begins to harden. You'll need all the hands you can get to make the balls as fast as you can.

The first cook can pop the corn and sort out all unpopped kernels. Pour corn into a large bowl or pan and keep it warm. The most experienced cook makes the syrup.

MOLASSES POPCORN BALLS

17

1⅓ cups light molasses
2 cups sugar
2⅓ cups water
2 teaspoons vinegar
1½ teaspoons baking soda
3½ quarts salted popped corn

1. Combine molasses, sugar, water and vinegar in a 2-quart saucepan. Cook and stir until sugar dissolves. Then boil gently until syrup reaches 250 degrees on a candy thermometer. Or, if you drop a half teaspoonful of syrup in cold water, it should make a hard ball when you pick it up.

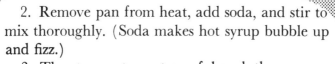

2. Remove pan from heat, add soda, and stir to mix thoroughly. (Soda makes hot syrup bubble up and fizz.)

3. The strongest, most careful cook then pours this very hot syrup over the popcorn in the large bowl. Both cooks can use long-handled wooden spoons to mix in the syrup so it coats all the corn.

4. While the syrup cools enough to touch, butter your hands. Or put your hands in plastic gloves or plastic bags so they won't be burned, and butter the plastic. This is a very good idea for smaller kids.

5. Shape the corn into balls. Work fast. Pack them lightly so they are easy to eat.

6. Put each popcorn ball in a plastic sandwich bag. Tie the top shut to keep the popcorn ball clean and dry for Halloween visitors.

popcorn

You can use cake pans or gelatin molds to make all kinds of shapes with candied popcorn. Butter or oil the molds so the popcorn won't stick in them.

Or you can form the shapes you want on a buttered cookie tray. You can decorate the finished shape with frosting, candy, nuts, paper cutouts, ribbons, whatever you can think up. This recipe makes enough syrup for a lot of popped corn.

5 quarts unsalted popped corn
4 cups sugar
2 teaspoons salt
1 cup water
2 tablespoons butter
¼ teaspoon cream of tartar
Food coloring (see NOTE)

18

1. Pop the corn. Put it in a large roasting pan and keep it warm in a 250-degree oven.
2. Combine sugar, salt, water, butter or margarine and cream of tartar in a saucepan. Cook and stir the mixture until sugar dissolves. Bring to a boil.

sculpture

3. Boil gently until syrup reaches 260 degrees on a candy thermometer. (If you test syrup in cold water, it should make a hard ball.)

4. If you wish to color the syrup, add food color now—a few drops at a time. Stir it in.

5. Carefully pour the hot syrup over warm popcorn. Mix with a long-handled wooden spoon to coat all the corn. Let cool until you can touch it. Press the popcorn mixture lightly into heavily buttered molds, or shape as you wish.

6. Let the mold set for a few minutes only. Then turn it over and shake out your popcorn shape.

NOTE: The four standard food colors are red, yellow, green and blue. You can mix them to make other colors. Red and yellow make orange. Green and blue make turquoise. All of them together make brown. A small amount of red makes pink, a lot makes red. Experiment!

SUMMER SUCKERS

3 quarts salted popped corn
1½ cups brown sugar
1 tablespoon butter
¼ cup water
15 wooden sticks

1. Pop the corn and put it in a large roasting pan. Place in a 250-degree oven to keep warm.

2. To measure brown sugar, pack it firmly into cup. Put brown sugar, butter and water in a 2-quart saucepan. Heat and stir until sugar dissolves. Bring to a boil and boil gently until syrup reaches 260 degrees on the candy thermometer. Or drop a half teaspoonful of syrup into a half glass of cold water. When it will make a hard ball, the syrup is ready.

3. Pour the syrup over warm popped corn. Mix with a long-handled wooden spoon until all the corn is coated.

4. When the mixture is cool enough to touch, butter your hands and form round or log-shape suckers. Poke a stick into each sucker for a handle. Your popcorn-sicle won't melt (but it might get a little sticky).

Easter Eggs

They're popcorn balls wrapped in shiny foil.

20

1 cup sugar
$\frac{1}{3}$ cup honey
$\frac{1}{3}$ cup water
$\frac{1}{2}$ teaspoon salt
3 tablespoons butter
Food coloring (optional)
3 quarts salted popped corn

1. Put the sugar, honey, water and salt in a saucepan. Heat and stir until sugar dissolves. Bring to a boil, and boil gently until the syrup reaches 270 degrees on the candy thermometer. Or you can test it this way: Drop a half teaspoonful of the syrup into a half glass of cold water. Syrup should form hard, but not brittle, threads. Candymakers call this the "soft crack" stage.

2. Remove pan from heat. Stir in the butter and a few drops of food coloring, if you want to tint your Easter eggs.

3. Pour the syrup over warm popped corn in a large bowl or pan. Stir with long-handled wooden spoons to coat all of the popcorn.

4. Butter your hands. When the popcorn cools enough so you can touch it, quickly form it into egg-shaped balls.

5. Wrap the eggs in aluminum foil. You can get different colors of foil from a florist. Be sure the popcorn egg is well wrapped if you hide it outside—or you might have soggy eggs.

HAPPY BIRTHDAY

2 quarts salted popped corn
¼ cup butter
½ pound marshmallows

1. Put salted popcorn in a large pan and keep it warm in a 250-degree oven.

2. Melt butter in a 3-quart heavy saucepan on low heat.

3. If you use big marshmallows, cut them in quarters with kitchen shears. Dip the shears in cold water every few cuts—when they get sticky. (If you have miniature marshmallows, you need about 4½ cups—and you don't have to cut them.)

4. Put marshmallows in the pan with the melted butter and let them melt over low heat. Stir occasionally.

5. Pour melted marshmallows over warm popcorn. Stir with wooden spoon to coat all the kernels. Let cool slightly.

6. Butter your hands and shape into 10 popcorn balls about 2½ inches in diameter.

7. For a birthday party, arrange the balls in a ring on a big round plate. Put candles in the balls to blow out.

Birthday Burgers: Make 20 patties of popcorn instead of 10 balls. When cool, put a scoop of ice cream between two patties and press them together. Put in freezer to firm. Serve these in cereal bowls.

Independence Is

CHOCOLATE POPCORN BARS

22
1 cup sugar
½ cup water
⅓ cup light corn syrup
3 squares unsweetened chocolate
5 cups salted popped corn

   1. Combine sugar, water, corn syrup and chocolate in a saucepan, and cook, stirring, until chocolate melts and sugar dissolves. Bring to a boil and boil gently until candy reaches 254 degrees on a candy thermometer. Or drop a half teaspoonful of the hot syrup into cold water. It should make a hard ball.

   2. Pour candy over warm popped corn in a big bowl. Stir with a long-handled wooden spoon to coat all the corn.

   3. Butter your hands and, working fast, shape the popcorn into candy-bar shapes—long, round or flat, as you wish. Wrap your candy bars in foil or Saran.

Making Your own Candy Bars

HAWAIIAN POPCORN BARS ★

23

1 cup flaked coconut
1 cup sugar
2 teaspoons salt
1 cup light corn syrup
½ cup butter or margarine
¼ cup water
1 teaspoon vanilla
2 quarts unsalted popped corn
¼ cup chopped candied pineapple

1. Spread coconut in a large baking pan and put it in a 350-degree oven to toast for 8 to 10 minutes. Stir it three or four times so it toasts evenly.

2. To make syrup, combine sugar, salt, corn syrup, butter and water in a heavy 2-quart saucepan. Bring to a boil over medium heat, stirring until the sugar dissolves. Continue to boil gently until the mixture reaches 270 degrees on a candy thermometer. Syrup tested in cold water should form hard, almost brittle threads.

3. Remove from heat and stir in vanilla.

4. Pour the syrup over warm popped corn, coconut and candied pineapple, and stir with a long-handled wooden spoon until all the kernels are coated. Shape like Chocolate Bars.

Popcorn Fudge

2 quarts salted popped corn
1 (12-ounce) package butterscotch-
    flavored pieces
1 (7½-ounce) jar marshmallow creme
¼ cup light corn syrup

1. Keep popcorn warm in a 250-degree oven.

2. Combine butterscotch pieces, marshmallow creme and corn syrup in a 3-quart heavy saucepan. Heat over medium heat until pieces are melted, stirring occasionally.

3. Pour the melted butterscotch mixture over warm popcorn and stir it with a wooden spoon to coat all the kernels.

4. Press the mixture into a large buttered pan—a jelly roll pan is ideal if you have one. Let cool. Then break into pieces.

Hey, don't waste that leftover popcorn!

Remember our Feathered Friends

Popcorn is a special treat for birds as well as for people. Pigeons, starlings and sea gulls seem to be able to eat anything.

Some small birds shouldn't eat salt so try to remove all the salt from what you throw out for them. Leftover popcorn should be ground for chickens.

Dog food often has a large percentage of cereal in it so your dog may already have an appetite for popcorn. Watching your dog jump for a popcorn puff will be fun for both of you.

SAVE SOME
FOR ME....

HOW TO MAIL AN EGG.

Or a glass dish, or any fragile thing.

Pop enough yellow giant popcorn to nearly fill the packing box. Don't salt it unless you know the person you are sending the box to will eat the popcorn. In that case, put a large bag in the box first to line it. Fill it half full of popcorn. Put in the breakable present wrapped or bagged in clear plastic to keep it clean. Fill the rest of the box full. The box should be packed just tightly enough so it won't rattle. Popcorn makes a marvelous packing.

What's That Thing Floating In My Soup?

25

A French idea:

Croutons are little pieces of toasted or fried bread that French cooks float in soup or mix into a salad. Use popcorn instead.

1. Sprinkle plain salted popcorn on tomato soup.

2. Season buttered popcorn with garlic salt or onion salt and set it afloat in onion soup.

3. Just before serving a tossed lettuce salad, throw in buttered, salted popcorn and grated Parmesan cheese.

4. Think up your own ideas and give them a try.

EXPERIMENT!

No recipe book ever can hold all the ideas people constantly think up or discover by experimenting. Flavors in food compare with colors in a painting. Soon a creative cook learns what flavors will go with others and how much to use. Be a bit cautious at first but give it a whirl; see what you can think up.

How about a popcorn Sandwich?
I wonder how it goes with
        Peanut Butter?

Let's sprinkle on some
            grated cheese.

We haven't tried it yet
            with Jelly!

Maybe I can invent
    A Super New Candy Bar!

Popcorn needs to grow in several parallel rows running north and south, rather than in one long row. This gives the pollen from the tassels a better chance to blow around in the wind and reach silks on all the ears. Without pollen no kernels will mature.

·To begin, stake out a plot at least 4 feet by 3 feet where it is sunny most of the day. That will give room for 3 rows 2½ feet apart, or about 15 stalks in all.

·Dig the soil deeply, at least 6 to 10 inches. It's hard! Ask somebody strong for help. If you are digging up lawn area for your corn plot, turn the sod under in the fall to rot during the winter.

·Most dark crumbly soil doesn't need fertilizer. Sandy or clay soil may, so use natural manure (with your neighbor's consent) or commercial fertilizer for plant food. Ask your county Agricultural Extension agent for gardening advice (listed in the phone book under "A" or "E"). Or the seed-store people can tell you about the best kind of seed for your area, and how much and when to plant. Do buy hybrid seeds for a good crop. Don't plant the popcorn from the grocery store.

·At planting time, two weeks after the last frost, hoe the soil to break up the clods. If the soil isn't

GROW POPCORN

well drained, make hills for the corn about 6 inches high. The hill rows can be 24 to 30 inches apart. Make holes 1½ inches deep and 10 inches apart in each hill row and plant 2 kernels in each hole. Cover with soil. Water if it's dry. If both seeds grow, pinch off the smaller one.

· While the corn is growing, water it if the soil is really dry and the leaves begin to wilt or curl. One good soak is best to encourage deep rooting to resist dry spells.

· Young corn needs your help in its race with the weeds. Hoe very carefully, not more than 2 inches deep, to cultivate the soil around your plants until they are tall enough to beat the weeds. Pull the weeds by hand that are very close to your corn.

· Let the ears mature on the stalks. When the leaves are quite dry and brown, you can pick the ears. Peel the husks back and tie the husks of 5 or 6 ears together. Hang these ears in a clean dry place to finish drying. The Indians braided the husks together attractively.

When the corn is ready for popping, the kernels will be hard and flinty. You won't be able to dent them with your thumbnail. But to be sure, test pop a few kernels. The easy way to get the kernels off the cobs is to rub two ears together.

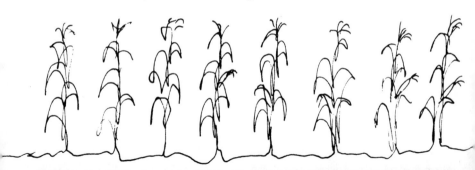

Carolyn Vosburg Hall pops popcorn just any time, using her favorite fondue pot. "Celebrations, disasters, or whenever you need a lift—popcorn is it!"

Now a busy artist, writer and mother of three, Mrs. Hall's good vibes toward popcorn began in childhood, when her own father stood at the stove. "We made a ceremony of it, with Mother collecting books to be read aloud while everyone munched.

"Now, my husband, Cap, and the children all enjoy being involved with my work"—Carolyn laughs —"maybe it's the popcorn!"

With degrees in painting and design from Cranbrook Academy of Art in Birmingham, Michigan, Mrs. Hall has taught children's classes at the Detroit Institute of Art, as well as adult classes. She and her family still live in Birmingham.

Mrs. Hall has exhibited her paintings and soft-sculpture stitchery in many one-man shows, receiving numerous awards. She is the author of *Stitched and Stuffed Art,* which shows the work of other artists as well as her own stuffed sculptures, many of which are life-size.

For this, her first children's book, she had the advice and taste-testing approval of her twelve-year-old son, Garrett.

And she worked in close collaboration with *Farm Journal* editors, who supplied production and nutrition facts, and perfected recipes in the magazine's Test Kitchens.

Farm families—the food producers of America—are eager to share with young people how their food grows and what it does for health. Popcorn is the first farm product to be featured in the series by Carolyn Hall and the *Farm Journal* staff.